Adjust

How to Conquer and Accept Change and Adversity Swiftly;
Stop Putting Off the Love, Money, Peace, Success, and
Happiness You Deserve Now

Original Edition

SAGE WILCOX

Adjust: How to Conquer and Accept Change and Adversity Swiftly; Stop Putting off the Love, Money, Peace, Success, and Happiness You Deserve Now

First Edition, 2018

ISBN-13: 978-1-945290-18-3

ISBN-10: 1-945290-18-8

Library of Congress Control Number: 2018948925

Printed in the United States of America.

Dedication/Acknowledgements

This is dedicated to all the people who are working hard to better their lives and situations, day by day, and in every way. Those who don't settle for mediocre. Perseverance and discipline pays off. YOU deserve to make your dreams come true and reach your full potential, and this book is for you. Enjoy!

Deep, humble appreciation to the Divine Source, whom I aspire to grow closer to every day, in faith.

Thanks to all who made this book possible. Also, to those who loved and supported me as I worked on getting it published. You know who you are, and I am grateful.

And, most importantly, to the readers. Thank you for taking the time to read this book. I hope you enjoy it and find something inside that resonates and inspires you in some way. If you find any of it beneficial please consider leaving a review. Reviews help more than you know. Thank you! Let's pour our favorite drink, find a comfortable spot, and get started, shall we? Our dreams and goals are waiting to be fulfilled.

.

Other books by Sage Wilcox:

Love Letters from Exes: *Proof That Life Goes On After a Break Up and Love Is What You Make It*

Get It Up: *101 Ways to Raise Your Vibration, Reduce Stress, Depression, & Anxiety, Increase Joy, Peace, & Happiness and Attract Abundance Automatically!*

The 2-Hour Vacation: *Let Go and Relax, Reduce Stress & Anxiety, Gain Inner Peace, and Happiness*

Until We Fall *(A Romance Novel)*

The Importance of Doing It: *How to Utilize Discipline to Get Out of Bed, and Make Your Dreams Come True! A Guide to Taking Action to Create Successful Habits, Reduce Stress, Anxiety, & Depression & Gain Self-Discipline, Motivation, & Success!*

Less Is Best: *Declutter, Organize, & Simplify to Reach Minimalism; Get More Time, Money, & Energy*

You Had Me at Re: Hello: *The Ultimate Guide to Online Dating, Including Tips and Testimonies*

Neuroplasticity and the Default Mind: *How to Shape Your Plastic Brain by Forming New Connections to Automatically Get Positive Results, Success and Prosperity*

Please visit her website at:
http://sagewilcox.wix.com/books
or
www.findyourwaypublishing.com

CONTENTS

Introduction   i

1 Suffering   1

2 Understanding   7

3 The Ego   17

4 The Forces at Play   21

5 Adjusting; True Testimonies   27

6 Responses   49

7 The Five Steps   55

8 Your True Nature   65

9 Easy Things You Can Do Right Now   71

Conclusion   81

About the Author   85

Introduction

Whether we know it or not, we are always adjusting. As you know, nothing stays the same. Things are always changing. Therefore, we are always adjusting. Working with people over the years, I've come to realize that hardships, heartbreaks, and hard times are a part of everyone's journey. This is a fact. I've also come to realize that recovery, healing, and restoration, either happens in one or two ways for people. They either accept the situation and adjust quickly, which helps them move forward, or they resist it, stay stuck, and prolong their suffering.

We can't control what others do, and we can't control a lot of what goes on around us, but when we learn more about the act of adjusting, then we can decide how we want to handle different challenges and changes, that will come our way, throughout our lifetime. In life, we will face challenges, and everything changes. We have to learn to take the good with the bad. And accept different changes that come our way. When we learn how to adjust and change our perspective on the "bad", then we can move forward to the prosperity that we deserve. Staying stuck holds us back from all that is good. It holds us back from better job opportunities, better relationships, better health, etc.

When faced with adversity, when faced with suffering, when placed outside of your comfort zone, the first thing people have to do is adjust and adapt. We can choose any number of perspectives when it comes to understanding adjustments, adaptations, and acclimatization. In this book, we have chosen to view it from the perspective of the human condition instead of one of the millions of other organisms and species currently cataloged. It is not just our physical traits that have been shaped by environmental forces but also the physiological traits, psychological traits and behavioral patterns that have resulted.

What exactly does it mean to adjust, and how do we do it? The irony in trying to understand adjustment and adaptation is not because we don't know how to do it. We do. In fact, we are experts at it and we are one of the few organisms on this planet that can adapt and adjust to almost any external force that challenges us.

This book is not about the various forces that cause us to change or the fact that we can change. The fact that we can change is undisputed and self-evident. A mere freshman course in anthropology and evolution will reveal just how much we have changed and we will soon realize that it is not us who change but rather that it is change and adjustment that eventually becomes us.

Adjustment is the response we give to any change or any new situation. Without change, the ability to adjust does not present itself. And without the ability to adjust we are not able to change. Without the ability to change we cannot improve. As such, when we can accept a challenge and take advantage of it, it's because of our openness and ability to change, and for the better.

But to balance that ability and propensity to adapt and

change is the proclivity to not move. We tend to call this laziness which also has other benefits. The state of lower energy results in us choosing the status quo as a good thing and shunning the prospect of change. Basically, it keeps us stuck.

When you are resistant to change the largest factor that is prompting that inclination is the body wanting to stay in its comfort zone. Some might call this laziness. Overcoming laziness, and thereby overcoming the ability to resist change is a matter of how much excess energy you have.

But it is not just energy from a present perspective, but also energy from a historical perspective that allows you to change or resist change. There are some people and cultures that resist change because of their ancestors. These people will carry on their ancestor's beliefs, and then the cycle continues, and it is a learned behavior that doesn't bring any benefits.

But the opposite is also true, too much change can unhinge a developing culture or a developing organism and cause it to not find traction. Things need to settle periodically before they can grow. If you look at the time of the Cambrian explosion and the times preceding it, you will see that the growth and advancements that were exhibited in the species were not continuous. The Cambrian period is referred to as a time of explosion. But actually, that is the true nature of our development. But we need moments of pause. That was the time that preceded the Cambrian. As such, as much as it is in our nature to evolve, it is also in our nature to pause. A sort of cosmic rest. This is a cycle that we need to adhere to. Even in respiration, you see the rhythm of activity and pause. That is the purpose and benefit of laziness. It is not the time to completely halt process but a time to pause.

When it comes to adaptation and adjustment, pause plays a big role as it is the time that genetic, and other below the surface, changes can be made to affect above the surface alterations.

As such is this not the prelude to the thinking that we are an organism that dislikes or is anathema to change? No. Change is what defines us and adaptation, adjustment, and acclimatization is what we are in response to that.

The alternative would have been to perish, and life is not in the business of quitting.

The environmental forces that we refer to are not just the everyday fluctuations in humidity, air quality, temperature and UV levels. It is more than that. It includes the supply of food, the integrity of the food chain, the balance of forces that stress our population like pathogens and diseases in addition to the sociological makeup of the place we live in.

If you think about it, adaptation is a very human characteristic, at least in the current form that we are. If you were to take a human being and transplant them from the equatorial region to the arctic region, there is a good chance they will survive. There are, of course, factors that would have to be satisfied, but the human body and mind can come together to make the necessary adaptation strategies and execute them. If, on the other hand, you took a polar bear and transplanted it to Africa, it is very likely it would perish. Plants are the same. You can see the gradual differentiation of plant life as you ascend the latitudes until you come to the Arctic tree line. Beyond that most species of plants are not able to survive. It goes beyond their ability to adapt.

But in human beings, we have the ability to adjust. All the faculties that we are endowed with, all the experiences we accumulate, and all the stories and lessons that are passed down and taught to us generation after generation, give us the will and the skill to adapt and face the challenges of new forces, or the same force in different form.

Suffering is the result of misunderstanding. Peace is the result of understanding. Adjusting is the bridge that takes us from suffering to peace.

We are always adjusting, whether we like it or not. Let's learn how to adjust easier and quicker so that our suffering doesn't linger unnecessarily.

Some of my books can seem a bit scientific at times, and this is because I feel as though we need to see all angles. When we obtain more understanding about a subject, the easier it is to adopt better practices in the future. Please feel free to skim over the entire book so that you can find the pieces that resonate, touch, and inspire you. You deserve more happiness and less suffering. Make yourself comfy and get ready to learn how to adjust no matter what others around you are doing or saying. No longer will suffering hold you back. You deserve to reach your full potential!

*"I can't change the direction of the wind,
but I can adjust my sails." ~Jimmy Dean*

~ CHAPTER 1 ~
Suffering

"It's going to start really interfering with your quality of life, your health, if you don't adjust to life as it's happening to you." ~ Noah Baumbach

Suffering is a personal phenomenon. It pervades each soul tirelessly, and is responsible for countless destructive cycles, and unfulfilling lives that could have otherwise had so much to contribute to this collective we call mankind.

Suffering is considered a potent external threat to the individual, and a demographic altering phenomenon to the population. Be it personal suffering or the suffering of an entire population, the experience feels real and the effect is nothing short of excruciating. In fact, suffering is almost always used to describe pain that is too intense to handle or pain that goes on for extended periods of time. That pain can be tangible and affect the corporal self, or it can be intangible and affect the psychological self.

Suffering can be personal, or it can be remote. We see the suffering in the eyes of millions of children who retire at night hungry. We see the eyes of their parents who, hungry themselves, are even more tormented by the suffering they imagine their children of tender age are experiencing from their hunger.

We see the suffering in the eyes of the displaced. Those uprooted from their homes and their homeland and cast out to the rough seas in pontoons; other perish across deserts on their way to a different land. Many end in refugee camps, more end up in slave labor, or some other form of flesh trade. Empathy is the conduit that transports suffering from the subject to the object.

Regardless of the issue, you can be certain that someone somewhere is suffering because of one thing or another. My neighbor wore his red golf shirt this morning on the way to the golf-course; that shirt could very well be a product of child labor. One of 73 million kids around the world somewhere, may have stitched that shirt together and in return made a few dollars that week. Is that suffering? Activists think so, and they suffer remotely.

In Kyrgyzstan, many coal miners are underage children who, in my opinion, should be in school - studying in the classrooms inside or playing ball outside. Instead, they work more than 12 hours a day, under the age of 12, and for their trouble, they make about $3 a week. We see the suffering there, don't we? Our empathy brings that perceived suffering home to us. We often apply our standards of pain and justice to a situation we know nothing about.

Then there's the whole swath of kids who didn't receive the toys they wanted, or the clothes they wished for last Christmas, or their last birthday, or some other holiday. They go to be, on Christmas Eve, after dinner, knowing that the next morning there will be no present waiting for them. It hurts, and they suffer internally. But most of us won't see that as suffering. Although the pain to the person feeling it is very real, it might not pass someone else's standard of pain while observing remotely.

It would be a mistake to pose the question that seeks to investigate which experience is worse. Which of those three experiences is real suffering? Surely it must be the kid working in the mines. Or the kid stitching the shirt for 12 - 14 hours a day.

Upon closer inspection, it turns out that the kid working in the mine, earning $3, gets to support his bedridden father, and his younger siblings and they may not have a lot of extra food at the end of dinner, but that family does not go to bed hungry. Same for the kid making the T-shirt. But the kid that didn't get his present, in this example, suffered as real as if someone pulled his little heart out. Pain is pain.

The young teenager who was heart-broken when her boyfriend of just 6 months broke up with her. Her mother, trying to help, told her that it wasn't real love, and to move on. But it didn't help one bit. The teenager's relationship was very real to her. It was all she knew and had been the most serious relationship she had ever experienced, and she suffered just as badly as anyone who had been in a longer, more serious relationship.

As hard as it is to understand (especially in the moment), suffering can literally be self-imposed. It is a figment of one's own faculties. The greatest suffering happens in the wake of a new event that adversely changes the status quo. Suffering has three elements that determine the intensity and perception. We will visit those in the chapters that follow.

When we are faced with events that we interpret as painful, it is just that, an interpretation. Some would say that even pain, when inflicted, is a figment of our memory. Because the moment the pain is inflicted there is pain, but after that, all that remains is the echo, not the real thing.

The handling of pain in this book is by no means meant to be callous, but it is meant to try to put it in perspective. It is designed to convey that pain and suffering are constructs of the mind.

If you take the position that pain and suffering need to be seen as pain and suffering, then you and whomever you influence is going to, at some point in your lives, build yourself on a world of hurt and sorrow.

Shakespeare, in Hamlet, told us that there is no good nor bad, "only thinking makes it so." If you decide that something is worth suffering over, and suffering requires that you act in a certain way, then no matter what the event, you will never see the opportunity in it. Further, you will never see that we, as a member of the living, have come this far, only by way of challenges. Or what some of us may call suffering. If you chose to see something as suffering, then you inadvertently see yourself as the victim.

If you want to become great, and I mean truly great, then don't head to your closest graduate school. Find a way to experience what you think is suffering and come out the other end. What you will find is that your character, your perspective, and your mettle would ascend to a higher plane. Because suffering is in your mind and when you can overcome your own mind, then there is nothing, and no one, that can ever stop you. The Romans used to say *"bis vincit qui se vincit"* Which, literally translated, means *he who conquers himself conquers the world.*

When you stop seeing adversity as suffering and you see things in a neutral light, you experience true transformation. You transform from a person of worldly senses and worldly notions and take on the divinity that only understanding of self in adversity can bring about.

In all of history, there has been no one great that did not first pass the baptism of fire. Half a millennia before

Christ, the emperor of the Arachnid Empire in Persia raised his son, Xerxes, who himself one day became a formidable General and emperor, by putting him in live fights with his army's fiercest warriors in life or death matches. Would you see that as any more suffering than the boy who works in the coal mine for 12-14 hours a day and feeds his family with his wages?

There is no suffering. Only learning and adjusting. Everything else is just a notion of the mind.

"I've learned to take care of myself. You know, I try to stay conscious of whatever my energy is at all times, really. I mean, I come home from work, and, depending on the day or depending on what was going on, if I needed to adjust, I'd just meditate, or play guitar, or watch some Monty Python."

~ *Brent Sexton*

~ CHAPTER 2 ~
Understanding

We are all familiar with the notion of suffering. We have all felt it at one time or another. We have all overcome it to live another day; and, we all have ideas of why it exists and what it means to the human condition. Religions and faiths have been erected over the many concepts and definitions and many embrace suffering because they feel powerless in its shadow, and few embrace it as the stairway to greatness. The question before you now is, in which group do you see yourself? In which group do you want to be?

The two notions of suffering are diametrically opposed to each other in terms of subject and, as it turns out, in terms of object. Off course, subject and object here are referred to in reference to standards of philosophy. Subject, referring to the person studying the matter at hand, and object referring to the matter at hand.

The opposition in understanding and in the meaning of suffering is a subject in and of itself complex only because the history of human civilization is long and full of trial and errors. Errors we and our ancestors make are typically long-standing and last for generations which can lead us to other errors.

Most of the people in this world suffer, simply because they haven't been taught a new perspective or a new way. They take any hardship as a personal assault on who they are and to a large extent, they see it as though there is a greater being, a God if you will, that has abandoned them. This feeling of abandonment results in pushback and people who feel this way end up doing the same to others. That suffering makes them bitter.

Then there are those who see suffering in the same way the wise sword sees it. You see, the sword, before it was the sword, was a block of rusty ore that sat in the corner of the blacksmith's foundry. It was deadweight, and good for nothing until the day the blacksmith put it in the fire, beat on it as he shaped it, placed it in the fire again, set it to the grinder till sparks flew from it, as he smoothed down the rough edges, put it in the furnace again, then shock cooled it. Until one day, it became a polished blade - a sword of great things to come.

The sword was better for the "pain" it went through instead of languishing in the corner of the foundry. If it had seen itself as being put to suffering, it may have cracked, it may have crumbled and at that point, it certainly would have been discarded to be consumed by oxidation and returned to the earth without even one measure of achievement or purpose.

Purpose
We all have two purposes in our life. That goes for everyone. One is driven from primal instincts and it's easy to accomplish, for most people, because of the internal pain and reward system. It helps get you off your feet to consume and sustain yourself. That's the first purpose - the primal purpose - to eat, breathe and multiply.

You are driven by feelings of reward and punishment by a biological circuitry that sits at the base of your brain. When you do what you need to do to fulfill your primal purpose - eat, breath and multiply, you are rewarded. You receive a reward of euphoria in your brain. We shall not delve too deeply here lest we stray from our topic at hand. But suffice to say, that the carrot and the stick here works very efficiently and has worked since the dawn of the animal kingdom.

If you want to know what it feels like, you can try a simple experiment right now. You know that the three primal purposes you have illicit punishment and reward - pain and pleasure for fulfilling or failing them. Let's take one of those purposes, breathing, and stop it. If you were to stop breathing right now, what would happen? Stop breathing and in under a minute, take note of how you feel. Imagine what happens when you are submerged in water and you really can't breathe. In about a minute, for most people, you would start to feel extreme discomfort. That is the start of punishment. You can breathe now.

The same goes for food. If you embarked on a commitment to fast, you will find that at the time of your next meal you would be subjected to mild discomfort. When you missed the meal after that the discomfort increases. And so on, until in a day or so, you will feel absolutely horrible. Not only has your primal brain not rewarded you after your meal, it has also resorted to punishing you for not eating.

In each case of denying your primal instinct, you will note that the resulting pain is different and prolonged periods of that pain, actually leads to what we all think of as suffering. The more you deny your primal instinct the more you suffer.

But it doesn't end there. First off, as mentioned earlier, you have two purposes. We haven't even got to the second purpose. Second, even when it comes to the first purpose, there is an echo that preceded the event. The harbinger effect.

You see, we have brains that can almost foresee the future based on past experiences and a simple set of cause and effect logic. We know with strong certainty, sometimes erroneously, that if you do A, B is certain to follow. You know, that if you don't pay the utility bill, the lights get turned off. You don't have to experience it to know it's going to happen. This knowing of what can happen is a form of looking down the road into the future.

When the brain puts the two together, it tends to worry. Worry turns to anxiety, and in the effort to ward off an existential event, it sends a flurry of punishment inducing feelings across your brain, in an effort to warn other parts of you to get to work in staving off the looming threat.

But we also have another part of us that, in moments of impending peril, freezes us and we don't know where to go or what to do. So, we bury our heads in the sand. We avoid the problem, in the hopes that it will pass us by.

But it won't.

Suffering begets further suffering.

We talked about having two purposes. One was the purpose to sustain life in our lifetime (and passing that life on to a member of the next generation). The second purpose was to use this life - the body that embodies that life and acquire the enlightenment that liberates our true nature. So far, we have talked about our corporeal life. That covers the first purpose.

The second purpose is less intense, and it is available to us if we chose - as opposed to the first purpose where we don't really have a choice in the matter. You see the second purpose is not something that we have to do, but something that we can choose to do. So, there is balance even in our purposes. One gives us no choice, the other does.

The second purpose, the one where we have a choice, is to find a higher calling of who we are. In doing so, we find contentment and abundance beyond measure. It does take some work, however, and it takes a measure of effort. But in the end, it is so worth it. Most people don't even realize that it's an option, and many more who do undertake it, give up. But to find your true nature is the purpose that most of us need to make, and the rewards are plenty. Finding your true nature is like the wave coming to the realization that it is just water. That is what we have to figure out for ourselves, as well.

For those who do not choose to take up the pursuit of their true nature, there will always be a sense of emptiness that is, in fact, the soul of suffering. Compared to the suffering of prolonged abstinence of food and air and progeny, the suffering without the knowledge of your true nature is worse. It may not be acute and intense, but it will be nagging and chronic.

When you are not certain of your true nature you will have this nagging feeling that comes and goes, and it doesn't quit. It doesn't quit - not until you find your true self. Instead, it quits as soon as you place yourself on the road to finding your true self.

The trick is to modify your first purpose to meet the needs of this journey you will take, in pursuit of your second and more important purpose. To attain your second purpose and to get to know your true nature, you need to be able to put a lid on all those primal instincts. Those primal instincts were put there to keep you alive and to get the next generation started before you knew any better. But as you get deeper into the knowledge of your true nature the only way you can get past the built-in circuit breaker is to deny many of the things that you thought were absolutely necessary to survive.

Now let's throw into this already complicated mix one more element of the human condition - ego, and you can really get yourself into a pickle. The ego is the largest antenna for suffering in most cases because it creates a situation that limits you on a number of fronts and you are not left to freely pursue the acts that will award you with success, as far as your primary motivations are concerned.

You see, as much as you need your ego to survive in the world where your primary purpose prevails, if you are to succeed in your second purpose, you have to abandon parts of your ego and take a leap of faith.

The ego is the expanded knowledge of your Self. Your conscious mind casts a net over all its dominion and calls it its own. At first, that dominion is contained within a very small area of the mind. As an infant, as your senses come online, you start to see more and more and you start to realize that attached to your consciousness are things you can control.

If you observe a newborn, you will notice how fascinated they are with their arms because that is one of the first exposers to control they have. Suddenly there is something they see that obeys each and every command it is given by the consciousness. Open palm, clenched palm, waving palm. All commands followed to the letter.

Slowly the consciousness lays claim to other parts of the body and takes responsibility for it. The more it takes responsibility for something, the more the ego reaches out to envelop it. Soon that ego stretches across space to include objects in its orbit. And possessions become part of the ego. It begins to define the original person in a way that can oftentimes be unhealthy.

But this is a necessary step in the process of growing. You need to build that ego up before you can understand what it's like to let go of it and keep going. It's part of the process.

"You have to be able to adjust on the fly, and that is what the great ones do." ~ Andre Ward

"I adapt, and I adjust to whatever environment I'm in."

~ Kevin Gates

~ CHAPTER 3 ~
The Ego

There is plenty of information out there that lays out the technical definition of what the ego is. But a lot of information that is out there is not relatable to many of us. Even when it does make some sense it feels almost irrelevant. We will look at the technical definition here, but I will try to give more details by adding on and going further in regard to what it means from an everyday, functional perspective.

One can decide on the scope of his or her ego. They can choose to be inclusive or exclusive, or any number of stations or stages in between. The ego presents a necessary condition for self-awareness. Without ego, there would be nothing to be self-aware of. The sex of the ego defines the extent to which the self is aware. If you are aware that you have control over your limbs, and that you have responsibility of them, then you include your limbs within your ego. If you know that there is something that others see as part of you, then you also end up taking those things on as part of your ego.

Thus, the ego is a function of three elements that you come into contact with. The first is the control that you can exert over something and if you do, then your ego covers that object. The second is the way in which your community perceives you and what belongs to you. That determines what is included in the scope of your ego. Finally, there is an element of imagination in your ego that inflates as a function of what you see yourself to be at some point other than in the present. If you see yourself in the past with no confidence, then that ego can become something of a low self-esteem.

When we say that an ego is a bad thing, that is an over generalization. It usually refers to the part of the ego that can cause us pain and destruction because it is so set in its ways. But we need our ego, so it's good to learn exactly what it is and how to use it to our advantage. If you have no ego, you would not be able to fulfill any of the things that your body has been presented with and, as such, you would not be able to fulfill your purpose in life. If you can't fulfill the bodily purpose, then you can't fulfill the second purpose either.

As such you spend part of your life building your ego and defining what it is and what it includes. Then you get to a point where you understand your ego better and choose to remove, train, or discipline parts of it that are no longer relevant to the journey ahead. This can be difficult, and if you're not careful, you will misunderstand this to be suffering. But it's not. It is just you kicking a habit. No different from quitting smoking, really. No different from any other habit that you got rid of. Looking at things from the perspective of the ego is also a habit and as much as it pains us to step away from it, it can be done.

"There are things I can't force. I must adjust. There are times when the greatest change needed is a change of my viewpoint."

~ Denis Diderot

~ CHAPTER 4 ~
The Forces at Play

There are three overall forces that surround us and relate directly or indirectly to the events that occur in our life. To better understand our place in this universe, we need to understand these forces and eventually understand how we adjust and adapt to cope, deal and overcome.

The Tangible
The first is the physical environment. This includes all the elements around us including temperature, pressure, humidity, content and contaminant, movement, space, vacuum and even time and gravity. You get the picture. These are the forces that are around us.

The Intangible
The second is psychological forces. These forces include the ones that have an effect on our individual and collective decision making ability. There is the use of widespread logic and academic learning to teach and communicate information. As we progress, we separate from other animals and primates in our ability to teach and learn. This has a significant impact on our ability to adjust and adapt.

The Force

Finally, the third includes metaphysical and spiritual forces. This is the realm of faith and spirituality. It is also the realms of higher understanding and higher purpose. Here is where we look past and beyond our flesh and the tangible. Here is where we perceive and understand the intangible to be able to make better decisions and have a better understanding of change.

The three forces can be further broken down for deeper study but for our current purposes, these will suffice. As with physical elements, all forces and motion have balancing forces. For every force, there is an equal and opposite reaction. In the case of the force to change, there is a force that resists it or a force to remain at status quo.

The forces in balance do not mean that there is no change, it just means that there is a slow change at a constant rate. When there is a change in forces and the balance is lost, then there is a jump towards the direction of the force and that is usually the advancement. Although, there are times in history where the changes have been regressive.

We define environmental forces as the external force that surrounds us and prompts our response in one direction or the other. The environmental forces that instigate and influence our response can either be tangible or intangible.

In the last one hundred years, a new force has also emerged that seems to form a formidable force, enough to qualify it as an environmental force. This new force has been at the forefront of much of the catastrophic consequences since the last ice age and this force has been something that we have had to contend with as a species.

This new force has been more pervasive that many of the other forces that have preceded it and it has been far reaching. It has been able to influence the weather, inflict the spread of disease and it has been able to spread the destruction of planetary responses and cause disease and destruction in its path. That force is no other than the collective force of the human being.

We have grown from being a consequence of nature to becoming an influencer of it. This has now resulted in beneficial outcomes as well as catastrophic ones.

Humans, as with other ambulatory life forms, are known to migrate in search of food. It used to be that once the food of a certain location had been harvested, the tribes would migrate to other areas. As such, food, and the way food is grown and in the way food is distributed, continue to exert a huge influence on the way we adapt and adjust.

Technology, which is a subtext of the second force described above, because it involves knowledge and communication, became a huge force in the way the human species subsisted and thrived. We have been able to find various ways of moving from the original hunter-gatherer origins to being able to convert from nomadic consequences of hunting and gathering to being able to cultivate the land we remained on. That allowed the settling of tribes. In addition, it brought greater food security to the people of individual tribes and it allowed settlements and cities to come about. The larger the cities grew, the more people, and the better collaborative efforts seemed to become.

With greater collaboration, came greater technology and we adjusted to the rapid pace of technological advancement as well. Not all changes elicit negative changes. When we face a change, we can adapt in both ways. Sometimes the effort required to adapt makes it a negative experience, and sometimes it gives us a positive experience.

Food security and food quality have seen change in the

ensuing physique changes. For instance, in Japan soon after World War II, the prewar conditions had left major shortages in food resulting in lower body weight and shorter stature. Soon after the property of the post-war era emerged and children had better food, partly in thanks to better wealth and better food distribution technology, there were increased growth rates and children and teens were on average seven inches taller.

The same effects regarding food can be observed in areas of Africa in the wake of the food shortages due to climate changes there. There was, in addition to an increase in childhood mortality rates, but also reduced birth weights and smaller stature adults. The environment we live in has a direct impact on us and we adjust accordingly to the status quo to embrace a new reality.

This ability to adjust is not only for times where we are consciously changing our selves. It is also for times that change our physiology without any conscious input from us.

Take for instance the change in altitude we encounter in an ascent to higher altitude. As the air gets thinner, our ability to absorb oxygen is challenged. The status quo internally is insufficient to keep us in a comfort zone and insufficient to keep us safe. The change, or challenge, that is thrown on us, then causes the body to respond. Without the challenge, there would be no impetus to adapt or adjust accordingly.

"It's quite normal to hear of a change and see it as a problem, but it's probably an opportunity, depending on how quickly you can adjust."

~ Jim Pattison

~ CHAPTER 5 ~
Adjusting; True Testimonies

*"Life at any time can become difficult:
life at any time can become easy. It all
depends upon how one adjusts oneself to
life." ~ Morarji Desai*

The following are true testimonies from others, who have had real life experiences, where they had to learn to adjust. Some quicker than others. I like to include testimonies so that the readers might be able to relate better in some way. We are all on different journeys, but together, we can share our experiences and learn from each other. I am extremely grateful for the testimonies that were submitted. I appreciate the time people took to write them and send them to me. I read them all and am so proud of all of the positive changes that are taking place in so many empowered souls. Although we couldn't include all of the testimonies in this book, they were all amazing and true testaments of the power within.

Testimony
1.

When Sage asked me if I'd share my testimony on how I finally adjusted to the fact that my husband left me, I laughed out loud. Partly in embarrassment and partly because I didn't know why anyone would want to hear my pathetic story.

Of course, with Sage's help, I now know that my story isn't pathetic. It has been a journey. A learning experience. But I wish I would have learned some of the tools needed to get through things quicker. I was stuck for over 10 years because my husband left me, and there was no need for it. I wish I would've known how to take steps to ease my pain sooner. I didn't realize that, in reality, I was hindering my healing. I was holding myself back from moving forward. I was causing my own suffering with my thoughts and then the actions that I took because of those thoughts.

After 25 years of marriage, three beautiful children, and two grandbabies, my husband told me that he was gay. And that he had a boyfriend. I was devastated. I was floored. I was shocked. I was angry. I was confused. I was sad. I was in denial. I didn't want to believe it. And I certainly didn't want to hear it.

We had just got back from a cruise where we renewed our wedding vows. Something we did every five years. We had a successful restaurant we owned, which allowed us to take vacations when needed. I hadn't worked since before we got married, and that was just a waitressing job, as we got married right out of high-school. I stayed home and raised our children and was now available to our grandchildren. My husband ran the business. We had a good sex life, or so I thought. How was this happening? How did I miss the signs?

Of course, looking back, there were signs. My brother,

Tom, told me years before that my husband had hit on him. He said that they were having a beer one night and as he got up, my husband grabbed his butt and held onto it for several seconds. Then he asked my brother "Do you like that?" in a sexual tone. I didn't believe it, but it made Tom uncomfortable and he had avoided us, for the most part, ever since. I had hoped that it was the beer talking or that my brother was exaggerating a quick smack on the behind. I mean we were Christians and my husband and I went to church every Sunday. *He wouldn't do that,* is what I kept telling myself.

So, we had just returned from our cruise, and my husband sat me down on the couch in our living-room. He said there was something he needed to tell me. He had been seeing a guy named Danny and was in love with him. He couldn't help himself. He couldn't control his lust when Danny was around. He was smitten. He was so attracted to Danny that he could barely contain himself.

Wait, what?! Come again? I don't think I heard you correctly? WHAT? WHAT did you just say? My head was a mess. What did this mean? Had he always been gay? Was he bisexual? That's not okay in God's book. He knew this, right? I understood that times were changing, but I also understood that God's rules were for our own good. God doesn't want us to get STD's or have to experience the heartbreak that comes from adultery. What about our life? The business? And who the heck was Danny? Would it be easier if it was a woman my husband was in love with? And how dare he tell me how aroused he gets in Danny's presence!

Long story short, my husband left me for Danny, we sold the business, and I got a job cleaning houses and tried to stay in the house we raised our children in. That didn't last more than five years as I couldn't afford it.

I remained stuck and heartbroken and in denial for over ten years! Looking back, I can't believe that I wasted so much time. Trying to win my husband back from a place I never thought he'd go.

Now, I can tell you with sincerity that I don't think I would've really wanted him back. We couldn't go back. How would I ever get any of it out of my head? But, for ten years, that's what I thought I wanted because I wasn't accepting the reality of the situation. I wanted my old life. I wanted everything to stay the same. I wanted to stay in my house. I wanted to cook only in the kitchen I had cooked in over the years. I wanted to keep my neighbors who I adored. I wanted the husband I thought I had. I wanted to renew our wedding vows again. I wanted the vacations every five years. I did NOT want change. And I fought against every single one.

I thought my husband would come back to me if I waited long enough. I thought he'd be able to continue to support me. I thought if I held on long enough to our house that he'd find his way back. I thought if I kept my life on hold and didn't date anyone, that he'd tell me he was ready to come back and that I was the only one he wanted to be with.

Because I was resisting everything, everything around me was a struggle. Everything was suffering, including me. My heart was broken. My health was a wreck. My relationship with my children was deteriorating. How dare they still love their father after all he had done to me? I knew this was irrational, but I was so upset and distraught. After several years my children grew impatient with me and we were no longer close like before. There was a huge rift between us. They didn't want to hear it. They no longer wanted to hear my sob stories about all of the horrible changes that were taking place in my life. I was broke and living in a tiny apartment and my car was barely chugging along. My children avoided me and when were did see each other all we did was yell and scream.

I cried and complained and resisted for over ten years

about what my husband had done. I didn't know what else to do. I didn't realize that there were any other options. I didn't realize that there was another way, and that I had a choice. That I was making the choice to suffer and stay stuck. I didn't believe that I had the power within myself to not only adjust, but to come out on top of this situation.

I had been to several counselors and although they were all very nice, I was not making any progress. At least, I certainly didn't feel like I was. It was the same old thing year after year after year.

Then I came across something Sage had written about the default mind. She has a book called 'Neuroplasticity and the Default Mind". I discovered the cold hard truth. Could I be the cause of my extended suffering? I say extended suffering because it is still hard for me to take responsibility for it. My husband caused my initial suffering, that's for sure. Or did he? After reading more about our brains and how they work, I discovered that I was getting something out of the suffering I was lingering in. It wasn't good, but I was still getting something from it. My brain was getting what it had been strengthened to produce. It was getting all that it knew. It was giving me what I wanted, although pain was the result.

This was all so new! Did I really have a choice in the matter? Was my initial suffering my responsibility, too? The enlightened gurus might say yes. Now, I believe that life will throw things our way, and they will hurt. And it's okay to feel hurt because we are human. We have emotions, but we can choose which direction we want to go in when the pain comes.

If we want to wallow in our misery (which is clearly what I did), we can, or we can stop right there and ask ourselves which direction we want to go in. Knowing what I know now, I would've probably still cried, because of the shock and betrayal, but I would have held my head high and said "Okay, you're standing before me, telling me that you've broken your wedding vows. You've betrayed me. You've lied. You've cheated. You're in love with someone else. You're gay. Okay, well, I am not gay. I am sad, but I will figure this out. I will get a lawyer who will help me figure this all out. (Something I didn't do before because I was so distraught and still under my husband's influence.) I will get my financial affairs in order. I will love again. This hurts, but I will be okay."

Now when things happen, or don't go the way I like, or cause me pain, I take a deep breath and release it. I ask myself (my inner being) questions. What can we do about this? Where do we want to go from here? What actions can I take that will feel better than this?

My progress has taken time, but thankfully, I'm starting to figure it out. Life has been much better and I've been much happier ever since I've learned how to use some positive and simple steps to help me move forward. I use positive affirmations, but only those that feel good when I read them. Sage explained how reading an affirmation that doesn't feel good, really defeats the purpose. So, I started only reading affirmations that make me feel good, excited, and alive inside. I ask myself questions. I keep a gratitude journal.

Ever since I've made these positive changes, my life has completely turned around. I have several friends and am a part of several groups. I go line dancing twice a week. I volunteer for a food pantry in my area. I am happy. I am healthy and fit. Something I never was in my previous life when I was married to my ex-husband. I met an amazing man. I have a steady income. I have a great relationship with my children and grandchildren once again. Life is good! ~ MaryAnne

Testimony
2.

Ah, adjusting. Why don't they teach this stuff in school? My parents got divorced when I was 17 years old and I've been struggling ever since they made that stupid decision. I looked back through my journal, the other day. Here are a few of my journal entries *before* I learned about this adjusting thing.

I can't solve anything.
I'm so frustrated.
Nothing ever works out.
I don't know why I even try.
I should just shut up.
Damn it to heck, I'm going to lose my mind.
I'm a mess.
I'm so stressed out. I'm not eating, sleeping, or exercising. I feel very discouraged. I should have been able to make something work. It's been years. I'm terrible.
No, I'm a complete idiot!
I'm going a little crazy.
I'm trying so hard, but bottom line is everything all went to heck.
Ugh, I just don't know. I have no money saved, etc. etc. etc.
I feel like I desperately need to bail on so many things.
Things have piled up like crazy, heat has doubled. I'm going to be paying off this year's oil bill for another two years!
Why did my parents do this to me?
I try and try but I don't get far.
I'm so frustrated because everyone is going to know I'm a failure and I look stupid!
And how shitty do you think I feel?
Argh, I'm gonna bust!
Whenever I think about my shitty life, I just cave inside.
Too bad I can't seem to do any better by everyone. I'm

sinking.

I'm really unhappy to be in the same boat, if not worse as another birthday goes by.

Things are all messed up. I am upset.

These are just a few of my journal entries before I realized what I was doing to myself. I'll admit, I'm still quite new to this new way of thinking but I finally figured *what have I got to lose*. Nothing seemed to be going right. Nothing felt good anymore, and if it did it was fleeting. I was negative no matter what anyone said or did to try to help me feel better. It was awful living in my skin! And then I started thinking on purpose. I started keeping track of the thoughts that were going through my head. I started journaling the thoughts, when I could, and was surprised at how bad my thoughts were on an almost constant basis. What was I thinking? Like seriously, what was I thinking? It wasn't good. It was like my journal entries above. It was constant.

I was also in a relationship with a married man. A man I had been seeing for almost six years. This, I know now, was totally affecting my subconscious mind. My soul. It went against everything I believed in. It went against everything I had been taught. It went against everything. I hated his wife for not treating her husband as good as I was. Ha! What a joke! Of course, I could treat him well during the short, sex-filled visits that we shared. Who wouldn't get along well during moments like those? I didn't have to wash his laundry or hear him snore or clean the toilet after him. And he didn't have time to listen to me complain or be grumpy or see me at my worst. Ugh, what a mess I was in. My thinking was a mess. My love life was a mess. My job was a mess. My life was a mess.

As soon as I started replacing my negative thoughts in my journal with positive ones, I could feel that it felt a little better, but not much. I wasn't seeing much change, *at first*. I even got frustrated at times because I didn't think anything was happening. But Sage kept telling me to keep at it, whether I believed it would work or not. And eventually, I felt a shift happen. Sage kept telling me that the things I put in my mind have a way of showing up.

I was coming from a place of gratitude more often. I was trying to see the good in my messed up life. I stopped blaming myself, and others, all the time and for everything.

I told my boyfriend if that's what you want to call him, that I wasn't available as much. I started doing things for myself and I found that I wasn't waiting around for him as much as I had before. As soon as I started telling him that I had other plans or that I wouldn't be home, he started calling and texting more. He was acting jealous. He was possessive but so charming and handsome. After being with him for so long, I did love him. Honestly, it was extremely hard not having him around. He made me giddy. And love making was out of this world. He made me laugh, running around in his underwear. He was a jokester. He made me excited as he fed me finger foods. He made me delirious when he washed my back in the shower. But it was always short lived. I knew he wouldn't leave his wife, and in all honesty, I don't think I would've wanted him if he did. The thought was always in the back of my mind, that if he could cheat on her, then he could cheat on me. I was too close to the situation. I was there when she called and heard how easily he lied to her. So, I stuck with it. I kept up with my positive thoughts, affirmations, and actions and I kept putting more and more space between us. He was angry. He was mad that I wasn't there for him when he needed me most. He even said he was upset that I wasn't satisfying "his needs" like before. He'd call crying. Which I had a hard time even believing. He asked what had changed. He asked if I had met someone new. He accused me of cheating on him. So funny to think about, now. And eventually, I told him to get lost.

I had to change my mind. I had to adjust to positive change even though it didn't feel positive. Change can be so hard. My married boyfriend was all I knew for the last six years. My negative attitude had become the norm. My feeling sorry for myself came so naturally to me that I didn't know how else to act, really.

I'm so glad that I decided to try to take another approach to life. It has been sweeter than ever before. Now, if I don't make time to read my positive affirmations before bed things don't go as good as the times that I do. Sometimes I'm just too tired to read them and I always regret it. I don't sleep as well either when I don't do the inner work that needs to be done. I've been trying to read them a bit earlier than usual. Not right before bed, but an hour or so beforehand. It only takes me ten minutes, so it seems crazy that I can't find a way to make time for it.

I will keep at it because so far, it has done wonders for my spirit. It's calmer. More peaceful. More hopeful. I will learn to adjust when needed and stick only to paths that will benefit my well-being and soul. ~ Janet

Testimony
3.

I was fired after 19 years of employment and I believe I was fired unjustly. I had recently requested that my workstation be changed because I was having some pain in my wrists and elbows. I just asked if maybe someone could look at it and brought it to my supervisor's attention that my workstation hadn't been reviewed in years and I wondered if the discomfort and pain I was experiencing was because of it. Any help would be appreciated.

Two days later, at the very end of the day, I was brought into the Human Resources office and told that I was fired because I wasn't getting my work done fast enough. And then I was escorted out of the building. I was humiliated and embarrassed. I didn't believe what they were telling me. I could feel my face flushing. It felt like I was breaking out in hives. I begged them to give me another chance and asked if it was because I had just brought my workstation to their attention. They told me they were very sorry but that I'd have to leave now.

I remember driving home in a daze. Tears running down my face. What would I tell my husband? What would I tell my kids? We lived paycheck to paycheck and because I had worked there for so long I made pretty good money for the area that we lived in.

The next morning, I felt like I needed to go to work. My desk was waiting. The desk I had sat at for 19 years. The unfinished projects I had piled up on my desk needed to be finished and I was the only one who could finish them correctly. With each minute on the clock, I would think about what I would and should be doing at work. 10 a.m., we would be all doing our morning stretches. 10:45 a.m. I'd be taking a break with my great friends and co-workers. 1 p.m. I should be in the department meeting going over the progress of my projects.

I got mad and decided I was going to fight this. Even though my state was a no-fault state when it came to employment, I was going to fight to get my job back. This wasn't fair! This wasn't right! How dare they do this to me! What did they expect me to do? Give up my entire career just like that?

I contacted a lawyer, and for months I fought my termination. I called Human Resources and threatened them. I told them they better not replace me or have anyone else take my workstation because I'd be back. I called co-workers and complained and told them to watch their backs because if it happened to me it could happen to them. I complained to my husband nonstop about what happened to me. Why me? Susie, who sat next to me worked ten times slower than I did. She was always on her cellphone and taking calls from her boyfriend, Billy.

My husband thought that I should start applying for other jobs. He thought the experience I had would speak for itself on my resume. NO WAY! I was getting my job back. I did not deserve to be treated this way.

Months went by and we were definitely struggling to make ends meet. We were charging our groceries onto our credit card. We were late on all of our bills.

My husband had a friend who knew of a great job opportunity that had just come available. They both thought I'd be a great fit. The position offered better benefits and pay than I was getting before and was closer to home. My husband said his friend told the owner of the business all about my credentials and that the owner said he trusted his judgment and if I wanted it, the job was mine.

Again, I said NO WAY! I was going back to work at my old job. I was going to go sit at the same desk I had for 19 years and prove to them that they made a big mistake. My husband was so mad that I passed up such a good opportunity. But in my head, I was going back to work, just to the same place I had always been.

Now I can see that I was stuck in my own stubbornness. I was not adjusting well to this new challenge and change that I was faced with. I was resisting, and my entire family was suffering for it. I had a negative attitude about everything. I was angry at everyone. I was slamming doors and throwing things. It got so bad that my husband asked me to seek help, counseling, anything.

After communicating with Sage, I started to see things differently. Sage told me that I needed to take responsibility for everything that was happening in my life. Including the fact that I got fired. This was a hard pill to swallow. At first, there was no way I would believe that I had anything to do with what happened. I didn't understand a lot of what I am starting to.

A couple of things I would've done differently... If I could do it over, from where I am now, I would've taken a deep breath and paused for a moment. I would've thanked HR for their time and for the 19 years they employed me. I would've looked up and thanked God for this new occurrence that was taking place. I would've said, "God, I have no idea what your plan is here, but I will trust in you and you alone. When one door closes, you open another bigger and better one." I would've gone home and explained the events of the day to my family in a positive, upbeat, and hopeful tone. I would've known that my children were learning from my example. I would've had the opportunity to prove that my faith was stronger than my circumstances.

My suffering and anger were mostly hurting me, but it was also hurting my family in little ways. Even little hurts add up over time and trickle on into the lives of others.

I believe God was offering the better job for me, but unfortunately, I missed the boat on that one. I bet God was a little impatient with me at the time. But once I became honest with myself, and forcing myself to have faith, (In the beginning it is almost like forcing yourself. It's a practice. It's forming a new habit. When you first learn to brush your teeth, or take up a new exercise program, you have to force yourself to do it. Habits take time and effort.) then things started turning around.

I could either be discouraged that I passed up a great job opportunity or I could have faith that another good job was in the works and coming my way. This was an opportunity to prove that I was putting what I had learned into action. My previous me would have sulked about the lost job for months. I would've talked and complained about it over and over.

My lawyer told me that I didn't have a case which just confirmed what everyone around me was telling me. It was time to move onward and upward.

I cried, I cried a lot, but I also sensed that things were going to be okay. Two weeks later, I ran into an old friend at the grocery store. She told me about a new venture she was diving into. It was for a company who was looking for people to work from home. They offered the same pay I had been making at my previous job and I could pick my own hours. They required a 40-hour work week, but I could pick and choose how I made up the 40 hours and which days I worked to do so. I applied and was hired three days later.

I've been working for this company for over a year now and things are going great. I LOVE the freedom I have to work from home. If I want to get my 40 hours in, in four days, and then have three days off, I can, no problem. I don't have to deal with the politics and gossip of the office and I can be available for my children. WOW! Why was I fighting to get my old job back?!

Life is grand, and I am very happy and thankful.

If you're feeling discouraged, know that you are only creating more of that same feeling. It's normal and okay to feel down, but don't stay down because you will get more things that will bring you further down. Recognize it, accept it, and move towards feeling better. Anything that is healthy and will make you feel better. For me, it was watching comedies, spending time with family, doing puzzles, and keeping a journal of happy thoughts and thanksgiving. Remembering what I am grateful for always makes me feel better. Keep at it. Your life and happiness are at stake. Once you form this new habit, you will be happier than ever before. ~ Tabitha

Testimony 4.

My twin brother, Jake, and I have led very similar lives. We grew up in the same house, played the same sports, went to the same college, and live within an hour of each other.

Here's the first letter I wrote to Sage when I was at my lowest point.

Dear Sage,

I'm writing to you out of sheer aggravation. I feel as though time is running out. Nothing goes right for me. Everyone is against me. No one helps me. Something has to give or I'm going to go crazy.

You see, I have a twin brother, and I know that a lot of twins feel competitive towards each other, but this is different. There's no competition between us. But I can't figure out why my brother's life has always gone so well. We've basically lived the same lives. My parents have always treated us equally and loved us the same. I just don't know what he is doing differently than me. Now that we are adults, and live our own lives, we don't see each other as much as we did when we lived at home, of course, but his life has been one success after another and mine has just floundered.

My mother told me yesterday that all I do is call her and complain. She asked me to stop calling if all I was going to do is complain. I didn't realize that's "all I do".

My brother has a great job, an amazing flat, a lot of money in the bank, a girlfriend that treats him like a King, drives a new Tesla, and is always happy. I, on the other hand, can't keep a job, live in a tiny, run-down apartment, can't save money no matter how hard I try, am in debt up to my eyeballs, have loser girlfriends one after the other, drive an old beat up Toyota, and am unhappy more than I am not. And no one is helping me. I thought my mother would help but she told me not to call her anymore.

I finally saved up money for a better car and then my ex-girlfriends fuse box blew so, thinking I would do the right thing, I paid for a new one and for the installations fees etc. and there goes my car money. Two weeks later the car offer I could have afforded comes my way and I'm broke. Then to top it off, my washing machine died. I do my best to be the best at my job so that I can get a raise and as soon as it is agreed, my back goes out and puts me down for a couple of days so that I can't work. I know I'm negative at times, but I just have the worst luck ever. I try to do everything I can and it's simply never good enough. Even when I go above and beyond to get there. Nobody appreciates me. There is a black cloud over my head no matter what I do. And our country is going to hell in a handbasket.

I'm surrounded by thousands of dollars of technology with gaming and musical instruments, and just a bunch of electronics and I'm miserable. As a kid, I played with sticks and rocks and was happy as a clam. What gives? My mind and body are so tired and running ragged...

I'm so frustrated all the time and one night, when I was drinking more than I should, and baring my soul, my friend Stacy told me that I should contact you. She gave me your email address and told me that she knew you'd respond.

I am hoping you can just tell me what to do. I am at such a loss and now my own mother doesn't want to talk to me. And if there's no hope, maybe life is just meant to be this way. We are just here to work and scrap by. Thanks for listening anyway.

Best,
Jared

To make a long story short, Sage helped me take FULL and I mean FULL responsibility for the words and energy of my letter. Sage started by trying to help me see what I was doing to myself with my words, to start. Words are thoughts in action, so that meant that my thoughts were just as bad, if not worse, than the words I wrote down on the page. I thought it was all nonsense at first. I wasn't buying it. It all seemed like utter nonsense. But my friend, Stacy, convinced me to give it a try. To give it a fair shake. I wasn't doing anything else but be miserable, so why not? So, I promised Stacy that I would do it. There were many times that I just wanted to say to heck with it. It seemed like complete rubbish. No one would ever understand my miserable life. But I promised Stacy (on my beloved cat's life) that I would do whatever Sage suggested that I do, and I wouldn't take any shortcuts. I got upset. I got angry and felt like I was wasting my time, but I did what I said I would. I am a man of my word after all.

So, I did as Sage suggested for 60 full days. To my amazement, after the 60 days were over, I didn't want to stop. I continued on with the exercises. My mom loved talking with me after, and the black cloud that had lingered over my life finally disappeared.

I didn't know that I was the main cause of my suffering. I didn't know how much power my thoughts and words had over my life. Over my reality. And I will never go back.
~ Jared

Testimony
5·

My husband fell in love with someone online, and abandoned me. I couldn't afford our house payment and all the utilities that went along with it, and it eventually went into foreclosure forcing me into bankruptcy. I had no real family, none that I could count on anyway, and I lost my job because I had a nervous breakdown and my employer was far from understanding.

We had two cars. My husband took the good one because I wouldn't have been able to afford it. He continually came around to get his things, with his easy new girlfriend stuck to his side. He was never allowed to come alone. Talk about being insecure. What, was she afraid I'd steal him back? Was she afraid she couldn't trust him? Was she afraid there was still chemistry between us? I can assure you that there was. She didn't know that he sent me flowers on my birthday. Or that we made love several times after he left and that it was amazing. She didn't know that he begged me to take him back, but I always sent him back to her. She could have him.

I talked to my inner being often, during alone times. I asked questions. I prayed like never before. I decided to pick myself up, dust myself off, and keep moving forward. I had to move so I sold most of my belongings. They were tainted with memories that would only hold me back, anyway.

I decided to get on a bus and continue on until I felt a pull to get off. And that's exactly what I did. I stopped in a quaint little town and came along a café where I had the most delicious lunch. On the corkboard outside, pinned up, was a crisp piece of paper with information on a place that just became available for rent. I called right then and there. It was a cute little cottage that sat beside a babbling brook and river. The landlord was extremely nice and helpful, not to mention handsome, and we became fast friends. We had many conversations and he helped me set up a website. With his help, I started a blog. I now have over 25,000 followers and am doing very well for myself. I have several businesses contact me and send me free products in hopes that I will mention them on my blog. And my landlord and I are now dating. He gets me. He has been a Godsend and I am so grateful that I didn't allow myself to get discouraged or lose hope. After we had been dating for 6 months he told me that, because of all his profitable real estate ventures, he is a multi-millionaire. He owned several properties in the town and in several towns nearby. He wanted to make sure that I wasn't dating him for his money, so he kept that bit of information to himself.

My advice to anyone suffering from change and hard times would be to follow your inner guidance. It won't steer you wrong. If you feel the need to do anything that is wrong or immoral, then please know that is not your inner guidance. Your inner guidance, your inner being, loves all and works hard at maintaining peace and harmony. Let all that you do be done in love. I was mad at my ex but I released him and never wanted anything bad to happen to him. I care for him as a person, but knew it wasn't in my best interest to stay with him. So always do what is right. What goes around comes around. But, most importantly, listen to your inner being in regard to your own wellbeing. Don't settle for anything less than you deserve. Treat others the way you want to be treated. Always be positive and kind. Never complain or gossip. Always find the positive. Love yourself as you would your dearest friend or relative. All of this seems so simple but for some reason, some people just don't stick with it. All I can say is give it a try. I'm so glad that I did. ~ Nicole

"You never go into a marriage expecting to get divorced. You go into a marriage expecting it's going to last forever, and you have a lot of ways you dream about the future. You have all these expectations, and then you have to adjust those expectations, and it can be a very unnerving, confusing time."
~ *Jenna Fischer*

~ CHAPTER 6 ~
Responses

To understand the nature of adjusting to the adversity that causes suffering, we can learn a thing or two from the process of evolution.

Evolutionary response to challenges faced from external stimuli involves three stages. All depend on the time horizon of the change. Persistent changes over long periods of time illicit generic changes and can result in permanent changes in our genetic makeup. For instance, in the event there is a change in persistent UV exposure, skin tones change. If there is an increase, then in time, usually across a number of generations, the skin color changes to compensate. If the changes are seasonal, then the changes are superficial and not genetic. If you stay in the sun for just one summer, the worse you get is a tan.

Genetic Adaptation is one of the slowest processes in the adjustment option of the human or any other organism's arsenal. It is also one of the most drastic as it is no less than a makeover, a new model to put it succinctly, of the existing organism. It takes generations for traits to take hold and once it does it is not swift to be reversed. The process takes time to propagate through the population.

To make the necessary adjustment, genetic mutations that regularly happen are tested in real world situations. If a genetic mutation survives in one generation, that mutation gets to transfer across to the next generation. The more that happens the more chances of that mutation making it across to the next generation.

But the thing about adaptation is that genes do not know what changes will work in the new situation. As such there are two ways genetic adaptation is executed.

The first is the random changes to the genetic code that allow the new organism to survive in the environment. The second is the constant changes that the body makes in anticipation of the certainty that befalls all of us, which is that we are always faced with change, and the body is always in the mode of change. So, in the event a specific event changes beyond what we are used to, then some of us, the ones that have the mutation to survive that change, or at least have enough of a difference in the characteristic, are able to weather the incremental changes and survive.

One of the elements of evolution that is sometimes misunderstood is the idea that we are reactionary in nature and that we react to the changes that occur in the environment. It is, however, the other way around, and it is because of a second element in the puzzle - biodiversity, that we are able to weather the storm.

Think of it this way. In a sample population, let's say that one third (let's call them Group A) carry a gene that gives carriers the ability to completely be immune to Virus X. At the time of the appearance of the gene, Virus X is not even in existence yet. In the same population, Group B has the gene that keeps the carrier well enough to withstand Virus A as it runs its course. And, finally, Group C whose members have no ability to withstand Virus A.

In the event Virus A were to descend upon that population, depending on the pathogen's profile and infection rate, it is likely that Group C is going to be adversely hit until a vaccine is developed. But Group A and B are going to be able to withstand it. The following generation, from this population assuming zero immigration, is that most of the next generation is going to come out with the gene that can withstand Virus A. Groups C eventually perishes in the event no vaccine is developed.

Eventually after one, two or even maybe five generations later, none of the people in this sample population is going to be of the same genetic makeup as Groups C. They will all be either A or B. And so now the dominant species is one that has adapted to Virus A.

Evolutionary responses are embedded in two biological phenomena - genetic mutation and biodiversity. There is also Natural Selection that is the external factor in the process. The genes that mutate can mutate in response or mutate randomly. That mutation could be something minor or something really important, but unless there is an external change, that mutation will not have the chance to flex its proverbial muscles.

When we look at the concept of adjusting, there are two separate paths that we can approach it from. The first is to look at it from a micro perspective and the other is to look at it from a macro perspective.

From a macro perspective means to look at it from a broad angle. When we see a population, we see how the entire population responds to a certain event. When we see it from a micro perspective we see the genetic adaptation and the ability to adjust from an individual perspective.

When trying to understand adjustment and adaptation, it helps to start with macro observations and analysis, then follow that with micro analysis. When you do that you find that the macro perspective helps you effectively isolate the perspective you want.

"We have to figure out why we see the world in different ways and then how are we going to adjust so that we can at least still understand each other."
~ Celeste Ng

~ CHAPTER 7 ~
The Five Steps

What we have been discussing, up to this point, probably seems a bit scientific but what it all leads to is a variation of the look at suffering. We can suffer in many different ways and all of it has one thing in common. Suffering is a notion of the mind. It is not a reality of your consciousness.

What about your body? Is suffering merely a physical thing that the body feels, or is it a psychological thing that manifests in the mind? The more you reflect on your own circumstances you will inevitably find that it is more mind than body. Most of what you feel, whether it is despair or frustration, happiness or euphoria, it is your mind that is responsible for it.

The good news here is that since it is your mind and the mindset that controls it, you can make a conscious decision to be whatever you want, whoever you want, and in any state of being that you want.

There are five steps you need to take to be able to overcome any adversity. All five steps are taken before the adversity comes your way, however. It's like the process of evolution, the mutation occurs beforehand in order to withstand the threat. In this case, you have the benefit of the mind and the mind has the ability to look ahead when it needs to, to create the solutions it needs.

These steps are the solutions you need to be able to overcome any suffering, big or small, trivial or existential. But there is one catch. The catch is that you will have to give up your present way of looking at life, and all that you find around you, and all that that entails. You have to surrender it all, and when you do, you will be stripped of all the notions that prevent you from seeing things the way they really are.

The five steps you need to know, and practice, to be able to proceed with life unscathed by the thorns of suffering are a way of life rather than a one-off vaccination. They are as follows:

Step One
Identify all the things in your life that you acquire, and have gotten accustomed to. This list will be dynamic. Over the course of time, you will be adding to the list and things that you give away or get rid of you can shave from the list. The objective of this list is to take inventory of all the things that you now consider to be a part of you but are not. These things are unnecessary to the development of your higher self and the attainment of true peace.

Every few months, or at faster intervals, give away, or sell things from that list. You will know when to do it. But as you get rid of the obvious stuff, you will feel a certain level of peace. And that will start the process in your mind that will get you accustomed to adjusting to having more of what is important to you. If you so choose you could even go as far as living a simpler lifestyle. Some people start this process and love it so much that they start living more of a minimalistic lifestyle.

Being a minimalist is not about living with less. It's

about living with peace. The more you crave, the more you desire, the more you accumulate. It all adds up and can lead to more suffering. And it can go on to rob you of the peace that you had when you owned fewer possessions. Some say true peace can only come when you have zero possessions.

Zero possessions is hard to do in today's world. It can be done, but it is not for everyone. Instead, you have to find your own zero. That's why you start with a list and discard things from there as time progresses. You will find that it is all just a matter of getting used to it. It's change. I've found that the more clients free up space, the more space they want, and they start to appreciate the lack of clutter and chaos.

Step Two

Make reflection a daily habit. An examined life is not worth living, or so says Socrates. You need to examine your life without guilt or judgment. Try to remember there is no right or wrong, only consequences. When you truly understand that the definitions of right and wrong were created because explaining consequences to humans is not easy, you realize that the concept of sin and punishment really are acts of wrong choices that bring about suffering in the end - the so-called punishment.

Just as you acquire physical goods, and that is what we sought to flush out in step one, in step two, we seek to flush out the thoughts and thinking you have acquired and grown accustomed to all your life. The reflection you perform will not cure everything in a matter of days, it will take months and maybe even years, but the one thing that you can be sure of is that the more progress you make, the more progress will come your way. The effects accumulate on a long-term scale.

A crucial part of reflection is the art of forgiveness. You have to learn that you can and must forgive yourself for all the things that you have done and all the things that have happened to you. This is not about taking responsibility. You've already done that. This is about telling yourself that it's okay. Forgiveness is a huge part of peace. When you begin to forgive yourself after you have taken responsibility you can do two things. One, you can stop feeling guilty, which is a total waste of energy after a certain point. Second, you need to be able to learn from mistakes so that you can improve yourself. Reflection and forgiveness are not two steps, they are two sides of the same coin.

Step Three

In addition to reflection, which is a matter for the conscious mind, you need to learn and practice how to meditate. Not you should learn and practice how to meditate, but you need to. Meditation increases your ability to understand the nature of peace and the true nature of who you are and how to accomplish what you are meant to. Meditation is not about becoming so calm that you dull your senses. If anything, the kind of meditation I am referring to is designed to heighten your senses and your sense of self.

In the first two steps you redefined the scope of your ego, and in so doing you increased the power of your consciousness. When you heighten that part of you and you then go into meditation, you will get results that will leave you invigorated. You enter the world of hyper concentration where what you think, say, and do, all operate on a much higher level than you originally thought possible.

Meditation is not just about reducing your brainwaves to the lower frequencies. It is not designed to put you into a state of false zen, where everyone is relaxed and oblivious. Instead, true meditation takes you into the region of gamma brainwaves where you get a heightened sense of self and a heightened sense of intellect.

Step Four

When you get to this stage, it's time for you to start affecting areas in your primal side. There are three areas that drive your primary purpose - to live and establish the next generation. Now it's time to fast and/or deny yourself the things that enslave you to your first purpose at the expense of your second. Your second purpose is to find your higher self and if you heed that call, you will find that some of the skills you need to get you to that point can only come from removing the habitual side of satisfying the primal needs.

Your task here is to learn how to fast. Fasting is one of the most effective ways to learn more about yourself and to gain insight into the state of things. The idea of fasting is not to starve your body of food. Instead, it is to calm your mind from thinking about food, to stop wasting time focusing on food, and to put things into perspective. Food is just a way to sustain your body and in time you begin to understand your true nature. Food is the source of energy and nutrition, not pleasure. By fasting you start to learn the importance of not seeking food for pleasure.

There is also something else that happens when you fast. You begin to heal whatever is not right with your body. Again, the idea here is not to become super healthy, but rather deal with the vagrancies and wandering of the mind, and in this case, it's about food. As you get used to fasting. You will notice that there is a certain appeal to working with a lighter stomach. Your thinking will be clearer, and you will be more in tune with things around you. You may have heard the saying to "stay hungry". By staying hungry you heighten your senses and make better decisions. By fasting you improve your intellect and your conscious processes.

Step Five

Release your propensity and natural tendency to expect things to go a certain way. We tend to go about our daily business with expectations of what will happen or what should happen. Expectation is faith's evil cousin. We mistake expectation for faith and when we do that whatever was supposed to be in our grasp, slips through our fingers.

There is a thin line between expectation and faith. Faith is the belief and hope in things unseen. Faith is also the will in you to make things happen exactly the way you ask for them. Faith is not passive. It is active. When you have faith, things happen exactly the way you want them to. But because faith is active it requires your effort and your action to come to fruition.

When you have an expectation of something going a certain way, what happens is that you just automatically expect it without any action on your part. You just sit back and expect that it will come to you the way you want, without taking any responsibility for the outcome. Expectation is not what you want to feel when you truly want something done.

In this step, after you have learned how to reflect, meditate, and fast, you will learn that you have executed all the action needed. And from here on, you incorporate faith knowing that what you need and what you have asked for, since you have committed your efforts in the pursuit of it, will undoubtedly come to you and you will have it.

These are the five steps you will need to end suffering in your life, and by example, you can be the person who ends the suffering, and potential suffering, of those around you and of those who look up to you.

These five steps are designed to be iterative and repetitive. After you get through them the first time, you will see improvements in your life and notice a different frame of mind. Then you will need to deliberately go about the whole process again. After some time, you no longer need to do them in sequence because they will all flow simultaneously. When you get to that stage you will see that a lot of what you're doing will come naturally and will yield benefits in real time.

Peace is your natural state. You have just gotten used to the way the world works around you. Things that are not important have displaced things that are. Definitions of what is pure and righteous have tainted what is natural. Remember our true nature is peace. We are supposed to observe to gain clarity, but it gets obfuscated by things which confuse us because we pay more attention to the primal nature of things rather than seeing things from the perspective of our true nature.

To find peace all you have to do is walk away from your primal nature (things of the world, jealousy, envy, etc.) and anything that promotes it. There is a reason it's called hedonism and you are doing all you can by following these five steps to move away from it.

"I think there's a time to work, and everyone has to kind of adjust. And then there's a time to relax, and be the mom or take the kids on vacation when you need to wind down. So, it's a matter of planning, and being able to map out your year or your week or let's start with the day. It is just being multi-tasking and being available."
~ Vanessa Williams

~ CHAPTER 8 ~
Peace - Your True Nature

Suffering is the symptom of a life that is out of sync with your true nature. The further you move away from your true nature, the more you suffer and the less peace you will feel. It gets to a tipping point when you find that the very thing that is breaking your peace is what you go after to soothe the brokenness that you feel.

It is no different from the alcoholic who turns to alcohol to ease his pain. Each time he reaches, he is digging deeper into the pit of despair, and climbing out gets just a little harder each time.

What we need to understand is that our true nature is peace. Peace is not the absence of an altercation or the lack of war. Peace is our natural state - it is our true nature. In peace, we find the happiness that we are designed to be and experience.

It is easy to lose your true nature if you are not even sure what it looks like and how it's supposed to feel. And you will never really get an understanding of what it is while your mind is filled with the trappings of this world. From the way we interpret our strengths and the way we punish our weakness, to the levels we go to, to satisfy and feed our raw desires, and to the way we place importance on the side of ego; these are a few examples of things that just bury us deeper in the illusion.

The question that many people ask me is if our primal instincts are so wrong, then why do we have them in the first place? That is a fair question. It is also very telling in the sense that our primal instincts were meant to advance one stage of our life. Our primal instincts are like the engines on a multi-state rocket. After climbing through the first phase, they are jettisoned, and the second set of engines are fired up. When the rocket reaches a new level, that stage is then jettisoned, and the final set of engines take over.

Each stage of life requires a different set of equipment and purpose to get to the point of where we need and want to be. But we can't carry or use the old equipment we had from the previous stage as that will impede our journey.

The same goes for our primal instincts.

Our primary instincts allow us to build up our physical body and allows us to find nutrition and develop our minds. As we develop our bodies and become stronger we are also given the opportunity to slowly build experiences and understand the world around us and the universe in general. The building of one stage, our existence, takes us to the point of adulthood and from there we then go into the stage of building the next generation.

By building the next generation we provide continuity and thereby fulfill our primary objective. That is why we have the desires to eat and procreate. That takes care of the first phase. We lose peace when we focus on the rewards that nature has given us, to get this objective done, yet abuse those rewards by not achieving the purpose. When we eat for pleasure, and not for nutrition and energy, we are feeding the pleasure system in the brain. This presents us with consequences that will cause one form or another of suffering. Diseases and ailments that look very much like punishments are inflicted upon us when we crave the pleasure and not the objective.

Once the objective is indeed accomplished, we are then free to go on to the next objective. That is to find the true nature of ourselves. The intellect that we gained during the first part of our life while we built our bodies was given to us while we built our minds.

Once we deliberately work on building our minds, we are able to find more of the truth by building our conscious presence and understanding our subconscious. Sometimes we go about it in the wrong way. We set up organized ways of acquiring knowledge and sometimes that goes astray. But the point remains that once we have built the body, it naturally moves us toward wanting to build, and learn more about, our mind.

Once the mind is built and the consciousness comes into place, we start to build even more on that and we hope that we get to this point before our bodies lose steam, before we run out of time. The body and the sustaining of the body was never the ultimate purpose - just the primary one. It is meant to be in service until we can get to the point of spiritual awakening and enlightenment.

When you see it from this perspective it becomes clear that the extent of the ego should not be stretched out too far in front of us. The ego is ideally placed around the center of our consciousness.

To return to the original thesis, there is no suffering unless we make it so and if we must be careful not to allow inconsequential things to blur our true nature. When we reach enlightenment, it is the same scenario as when the wave that was originally concerned with how high, how fast and how curved it was, as it rushed to the beach, finally realizes that in the end, as it was in the beginning, the wave is and always will be just water.

"If you take everything personally and to heart, it will tear you apart. Take criticism, learn, adjust, and move on."
~Johnny Iuzzini

~ Chapter 9 ~
Easy Things You Can Do Right Now

Because things are always changing, we have to decide how we are going to adjust to these changes.

Some of the most popular changes that take place are:

New jobs
Breakups
Divorces
Job losses
A new move
A new school
Going to college
Empty Nest Syndrome
The death of a loved one
Health issues
Accidents
A new baby

New parents are adjusting to parenthood just as much as their new baby is adjusting to life outside the womb. Most babies sleep a lot during their first few months of life, so parents can slowly adjust to having this precious bundle to care for. As days go on, the baby sleeps less, and parents adjust to this change, as well. Parents are constantly having to adjust as their children get older, too. The terrible twos and the teenage years are a couple of examples of how adjustment takes place for all concerned. I've had several parents suffer miserably as their teenage children find their independence. It can be tough and letting go takes discipline and practice.

Parenting is an example of having to adjust to a different lifestyle than we previously had before and that kind of adjusting just kind of naturally takes place over time.

Adjusting to an unexpected change can be more challenging. But learning a few easy techniques, when faced with something you didn't want or expect, can make all the difference in the world.

Why do some people not cope well, while others thrive under the same exact circumstances? Those who thrive during changes and challenges view all experiences as a part of life; a part of being human. Instead of seeing change as a negative thing, or themselves as a victim of circumstance, they look for opportunities in the situation.

Here are a few easy things you can do right now to adjust easier and quicker to unexpected changes.

- *Analyze the situation.*
  Ask yourself questions. What is happening? What can I do with this new information I've been given? What steps can I take knowing what I now know? What do I need to do to take care of myself in this situation? Try to take a step back and go from there.

- *Change your perception*
  This can be tough at first, so you may have to

come back to it. But try to see the situation from the other person's point of view. Or from an outside perspective. I like to call this "Be the witness". Close your eyes and see yourself floating above the room looking down at yourself. See yourself as a person going through something. Knowing that all will be okay. All will work out, because it always does.

- *Acknowledge how you feel*
Be patient with yourself. It's okay to feel sad, or scared, or uncertain. These emotions make us human. What's not okay is to stay stuck in these emotions. It's okay to cry if you feel like crying. We were given tears to let them out. Cry when you need to, but don't stay stuck there. Once you're done, pick yourself up and try to do things that will brighten your spirit. Do your favorite thing. Watch a funny movie. Emotions can be great gages as to where we want to go, so acknowledging how you feel will help you accept the situation even more.

- *Find the lesson in it, find the good*
Over the years, I've found that those who adjust to adversity and change the easiest, are those who possess the quality of finding the good in every situation. Life is always helping us grow and prosper. See if you can find at least one lesson that will ultimately help you grow in some way. For example, a dear friend of mine lost a child at a young age. She said her loss helped her become a more compassionate person. She also said that she sees life completely different now. Through a new light, so to speak. She is grateful for every single day – something she feels she took for granted beforehand.

- *Make time for you – Exercise, relax, breathe*

Take at least 30 minutes a day (more if time allows) to do things that will benefit your mind, body, and soul. Exercise is great at relieving stress, boosts the mood, releases toxics, improves circulation, and is good for your heart. Yoga or just plain stretching is great for your body. Relaxation techniques and meditation are great ways to connect to your inner being who wants to guide you in the right direction if you will take the time to connect and listen. Take a bath, listen to a guided meditation. Relax. And make sure to take some deep breaths every now and then. Breathe in for a count of five (expanding and filling your belly), hold for a count of five, and breathe out for a count of five.

- *Create a plan, make lists, get prepared*
  What can you do right now to move in a positive direction? What steps can you take to help this transition be less painful, or go more smoothly? What do you want to happen? Make a list of clear-cut, short term goals that are attainable.

- *Talk to others, reach out*
  Talk to others who have been in a similar situation as you. Join support groups if necessary. Knowing that you are not alone, and that others have gotten through, can help tremendously.

- *Journal*
  Get your feelings on paper. Create a gratitude journal as well. Writing things down helps us process them. And gratitude journals have been known to transform lives for the better.

- *Focus, focus, focus*
  Focus on your values, your moral code, and your goals. Focus on positive things only. Do not

focus on your fears and insecurities. Do not allow yourself to be negative. I listened to bigtime motivational speaker, Anthony Robbins, say that we need to be positive for at least 21 days straight, and if we find ourselves being or saying something negative then we need to completely start over until we can say that we did it for 21 days. Can you not say or think anything negative for 21 days? Get a calendar and mark off the days. Start over if necessary. Focus. Become aware of what you are thinking. Journal your thoughts. Thoughts become things. Our thoughts create our reality.

- *Visualize*
  Take the time to stop and close your eyes. Practice using your creative mind. The more you practice the art of visualization, the better you will become at it. See what you want in your mind's eye. See it in detail. See yourself being and doing and having exactly what you want. See yourself facing this change with dignity and grace. See what your wearing, hear what you're saying, visualize how you want others to react to you. There are so many books on the power of visualization, be sure to be utilizing this inner power that we all have access to.

- *Don't' blame or complain*
  Even if someone else wronged you, that viewpoint is only going to hold you back. Release and let go. Take full responsibility for how you are going to react. Take full responsibility for finding the opportunity or lesson in the situation. Blaming and hating others only blocks the flow of wellness that the Universe wants to pour out on us. Disliking someone only hurts you. Positive affirmations can help with this a lot. Read this every morning, noon, and night

and feel the power and release behind it.

All things that have offended me, I forgive. Things past, things present, things future, I forgive. I forgive myself and everything and everybody who can possibly need forgiveness. I forgive positively everyone. I am free, and they are fee too. All things are cleared up between us now and forever. I loose and let go, I let go and grow.

- *Release expectations*
  William Shakespeare said: *"Expectation is the root of all* heartache.*"*
  Or another way to put it:
  "Peace begins when expectation ends." ~ Sri Chinmoy
  Releasing expectations takes practice, but once you learn not to expect certain outcomes or behaviors from others, you will sense a freedom like no other. When you find yourself thinking something should go a certain way, remind yourself that there are more perspectives available, and that it's okay if things don't go according to the way you wish that they would.

- *Remember you are in control of your attitude*
  Zig Ziglar said: *"Your attitude, not your aptitude, will determine your altitude."*
  Your attitude will determine how far and high you go. Train your brain to have a positive attitude, no matter what. You are in complete control over your own attitude. Sometimes it doesn't feel like it, especially in the heat of the moment, but you do. If you stop and pause in those moments, collect your thoughts (because remember thoughts become things and words are just thoughts in action), and then decide what attitude you want to take. You are always

deciding. Choose to have a good attitude. You will reap the benefits.

- *Remind yourself of past successes*

  You have certainly been through changes and challenges before. Remind yourself that you weathered the storm before in different situations and you can and will be able to handle more if they come your way. Remind yourself of the strength you have within. You are an infinite being. You are strong. You are capable.

- *Positive affirmations*

  I can't stress the importance of saying positive affirmations out loud. When you say positive affirmations, you are literally reprograming your subconscious mind. You are taking control and forming new beliefs that will help you thrive in all areas of your life. There are several resources online for finding positive affirmations, but the key is finding the ones that feel good when you say them. Play around with several and jot down your favorites. The ones that resonate with you. I am affirmations are extremely powerful, as well.

  I am creative
  I am smart
  I am successful
  I am forgiving
  I am healthy, wealthy, and wise

  The key is to say these as often as you can. Saying them in front of a mirror is powerful as well. People often ask me how long they have to do it. I tell them, your current programming happened over your entire lifetime, so ideally you should make this a habit like brushing your teeth. A new habit or belief can be formed within 21 to 60 days, so do that, at least.

The pessimist complains about the wind;
the optimist expects it to change; the
realist adjusts the sails.
~William Arthur Ward

Conclusion

All of history has but one lesson to teach us. From the shifting continents of our then young planet to the changes in climate; and advances in thought and understanding; everything about our evolutionary history, in fact, everything about our evolution, has been about change, and we have had to adjust and adapt to that change.

That makes our very existence, a product of change. On the other side of that coin, we happen to also be an agent of change for the environment around us and the occupants of that environment. If change were the cause, adjustment would be the extended effect. They go hand in hand and one without the other would either be impossible to imagine.

The evidence of our ability to change, in fact, our dependence on it, is found in all our physical features and the fact that a human being can be found in every climate zone on earth. We started out at the tropical latitudes and made our way to the extreme colds on either side of the equator. All the while, as we migrated, our bodies adapted and adjusted to the climate changes across the latitudes. Generations later, some of our features changed as well. We went from the darker tanned skinned to lighter skin because of the change in the amount and intensity of sunlight we were exposed to. We adapted, and we adjusted how our bodies adapted to the new environment.

But will this history of affinity and defining inclusion, external change and internal adjustment become the pair of phenomenon's that we explicitly endure and acknowledge? Yet, we seem surprised that it is there. When change happens, we resist. Why?

Is it that we are incapable of realizing that all things change? Are we incapable of realizing that things manifest in one way today and in another way tomorrow? Have we forgotten that if it weren't for change, we wouldn't exist? Yes, evidence would point to the affirmative on all counts.

While our desire to be bigger, better and faster drives us to be the agent of change, it is our fears (and our habit of staying in our comfort zone) that impede our exploration forward. These heavy anchors weigh us down because we are not willing to change and adjust. On one hand, our anchors can move us forward to innovate, but on the other hand, they can also lead us towards shying away, and not take action.

Even though we human beings are the personification of adaptation and adjustment, we seem to consciously adapt and adjust poorly. The reason for this is that the balance of power between maintaining the status quo and changing the status quo comes down to the battle between the two most powerful categories of forces. On the one side, you have the subconscious that is acceptable and amenable to change, while on the other side you have the conscious mind that is stubbornly glued to the moment and not willing to change or move past a certain point in time.

Within you are the push and pull that keeps humanity from speeding off recklessly into the future and falling aimlessly into the past.

That same characteristic within each of us that keeps us anchored in the present moment is also the same fiber of ourselves that is resistant to change and prevents us at every turn to adjusting from our past state to our present state. That poses a conundrum, how do we unlock one and not the other?

We are hedonism truly the embodiment of adjustment. The ability to adjust is in our nature, but so is the ability to stay the course. We get to choose.

Suffering is personal because it is tied to how we see things and it is tied to the consequences of our choices. Only we can liberate ourselves from the binds that hold us to it. We have the innate power to adjust and we can use that as the bridge to get from suffering to peace. Adjustments are temporary to dynamic situations and they serve a purpose.

Our ultimate goal, however, is to find our true self. But we can't find our true self right out of the gate as infants. We need to go through changes and in going through these changes we are given the ability to adjust. Suffering is just the signal to adjust, adapt, and to roll with the punches, or go with the flow. Nothing is ever permanent; it is always in our minds and in our perspective. But when we find our true nature, all suffering will cease, and peace will reign.

About Sage Wilcox

Sage lives in the United States and is a certified energy healer. Sage enjoys giving advice to clients, friends, and family on healing, love, and relationships. Sage also enjoys studying human behavior, reading, writing, being outdoors, and enhancing her relationships with others.

Other books by Sage:

Love Letters from Exes: *Proof That Life Goes On After a Break Up and Love Is What You Make It*

Get It Up: *101 Ways to Raise Your Vibration, Reduce Stress, Depression, & Anxiety, Increase Joy, Peace, & Happiness and Attract Abundance Automatically!*

The 2-Hour Vacation: *Let Go and Relax, Reduce Stress & Anxiety, Gain Inner Peace, and Happiness*

Until We Fall *(A Romance Novel)*

The Importance of Doing It: *How to Utilize Discipline to Get Out of Bed, and Make Your Dreams Come True! A Guide to Taking Action to Create Successful Habits, Reduce Stress, Anxiety, & Depression & Gain Self-Discipline, Motivation, & Success!*

Less Is Best: *Declutter, Organize, & Simplify to Reach Minimalism; Get More Time, Money, & Energy*

You Had Me at Re: Hello: *The Ultimate Guide to Online Dating, Including Tips and Testimonies*

Neuroplasticity and the Default Mind: *How to Shape Your Plastic Brain by Forming New Connections to Automatically Get Positive Results, Success and Prosperity*

Please visit her website at:
http://sagewilcox.wix.com/books
or
www.findyourwaypublishing.com

Would you please consider leaving reviews, online, for my books? Reviews help more than you know, and do not have to be long; a few sentences will do. Thank you very much for your time and consideration. I am sincerely grateful.

Wishing many blessings to you and yours,

~Sage

Disclaimer

The purpose of this book is for entertainment purposes only. This book is designed to provide information and motivation to our readers. The content is the sole expression and opinion of its author, and not necessarily that of the publisher. The testimonies contained in this book are from contributors and are the contributor's recollections of their experiences. This is a work based on opinions, recollections, and true events, however, names, characters, businesses, places, and incidents are either the products of the authors' imaginations or used in a fictitious manner. Any resemblance to actual persons, living or dead, businesses, companies, events, locales, or actual events is entirely coincidental. This book is not intended nor is it implied to be a substitute for professional medical advice, and any medical advice and any medical information contained in this book is not intended to be diagnostic or treatment in any way. The author and publisher are not engaged in rendering medical, psychological, legal, or any other professional services. If medical, psychological or other expert assistance is required, please talk to your physician and locate the services of a competent professional. The author and publisher shall have neither liability nor responsibility to any person or entity with respect to any loss or damage caused, or alleged to have been caused, directly or indirectly, by the information contained in this book. Neither the publisher nor the individual author(s) shall be liable for any physical, psychological, emotional, financial, or commercial damages, including, but not limited to, special, incidental, consequential or other damages. Our views and rights are the same: You are responsible for your own choices, actions, and results. If you do not wish to be bound by the above, you may return this book along with a copy of the receipt to the publisher for a full refund.

www.ingramcontent.com/pod-product-compliance
Lightning Source LLC
Chambersburg PA
CBHW060512280326

41933CB00014B/2939